A
Passion for Personal
and
Vocational Excellence

*A Dozen Bellarmine University
Baccalaureate Exhortations*

Rev. J. Ronald Knott, D.Min.

Sophronismos Press
Louisville, Kentucky

A Passion for Personal and Vocational Excellence:
A Dozen Bellarmine University Baccalaureate Exhortations

For information address:
Sophronismos Press
1271 Parkway Gardens Court #106
Louisville, Kentucky 40217

Cover Design & Book Layout:
Tim Schoenbachler

First Printing: September 2015

ISBN: 978-0-9962445-1-0

Also by J. Ronald Knott

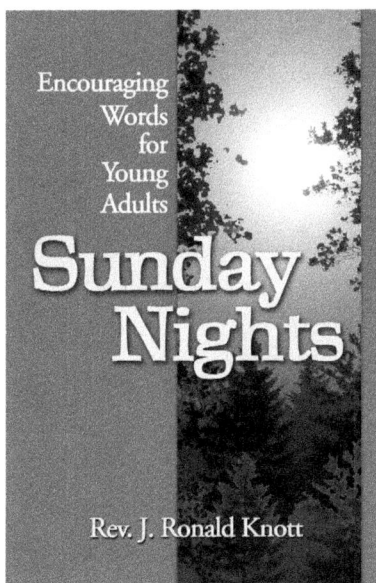

Encouraging Words for Young Adults

Sunday Nights

Rev. J. Ronald Knott

The Lord Is Close to the Brokenhearted

Five Years of Encouragement at *Blue Christmas Masses* from Rev. J. Ronald Knott

Our Lady of the Woods Chapel
Bellarmine University

A collection of Sunday night homilies given at Our Lady of the Woods Chapel on the campus of Bellarmine University.

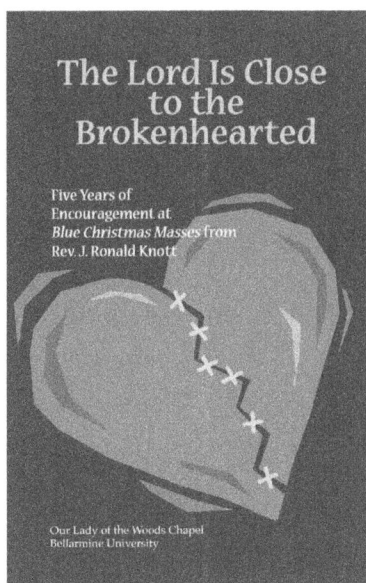

A collection of homilies given at *Blue Christmas Masses* at Our Lady of the Woods Chapel on the campus of Bellarmine University.

To purchase these books as well as eBook and printed editions of other books by Father Knott, go to:
www.ronknottbooks.com

View his blog at: www.FatherKnott.com

DEDICATION

To
Melanie Prejean Sullivan
Faithful Campus Ministry Partner
for Fifteen Years

Table of Contents

FOREWORD

I have always enjoyed being around young adults as a priest. I especially enjoy those Catholic young adults who are still active in the Church. Unlike some of their peers who, at least for now, have thrown out the baby with the bath water, they have been tenacious in trying to internalize their religious upbringing. No longer resisting that religious upbringing, they have begun the challenging process of making the faith of their parents their own personal faith. I find them deeply spiritual, often ravenously so. They want to know God, love God, and serve God; and to feel valued and appreciated by the Church.

One of the many choices facing young adults in every age is whether to embrace or discard all or part of their religious upbringing. Most of them, especially during the turmoil of adolescence, go through some degree of rebellion. Some do not make it through that period of sorting and sifting, but many do make it and begin their own personal faith journeys in whatever faith community to which they belong.

To borrow some words from Shakespeare, they "unthread the rude eye of rebellion and welcome home again discarded faith." It is to this group that I have especially addressed this collection of homilies delivered at Baccalaureate Masses over the last fifteen years.

I want to offer a special thanks to Dr. Joseph J. McGowen, President of Bellarmine University, who invited me to do campus ministry at Bellamine University in the

Fall of 1999. His invitation has provided me with an opportunity to accompany many fine young adults, students of Bellarmine University, as well as visiting young adults from around the diocese and around the country in their personal faith journeys.

Fr. Ronald Knott

August 16, 2015

Be Good and Good At It

May 10, 2003

I am the good shepherd, and I know mine and mine know me. I have other sheep that do not belong to this fold. These also must I lead.

JOHN 10

I was born and raised in St. Theresa Parish down in Meade County. One of my earliest childhood memories is the scene of my pastor, Father Felix J. Johnson, walking through the parish cemetery, dressed in coveralls and carrying a bucket of water in each hand, to water the sheep who grazed among the tombstones. He wasn't trying to be romantic, he was just doing what needed to be done to save money in a country parish that did not have a lot of money to waste. The cemetery needed mowing and mutton was served at the parish picnic every August. Looking back you have to admit that he was pretty ingenious.

The word "pastor" is the Latin word for a "shepherd." Father Johnson was not only a "shepherd" in the literal sense, he was our "shepherd" in the spiritual sense. Just as he fed and protected his flock of sheep, he fed and protected us as his parishioners for many, many years. He could be tough. He put up with no religious nonsense from his flock, but people loved and respected him nonetheless. I always think of him when I read the passages about Jesus, the "good shepherd."

Not only was he a "good shepherd," he was also a master carpenter, bricklayer, draftsman and "water-witch."

He was called on by parishioners for help in designing buildings and to find the best places to drill for water wells. As a master carpenter and bricklayer he was the main carpenter for the rectory, convent, parish hall and school, laying most of the brick himself. As our "pastor," he was "good" and "good at it."

I doubt seriously that many of you will be going into the "shepherd" business after graduation. If that were true you would have attended the "grazing school" offered by the University of Kentucky College of Agriculture or you would have asked me for an application to the seminary for the Fall. Since most of you will be going into other professions, what bits of wisdom can be gleaned for you from today's reading about the "good shepherd?" What message could possibly be relevant for those of you who are graduating with degrees in business, nursing, liberal arts and education?

I am the good shepherd.

There are two words in Greek for "good," *agathos* and *kalos*. *Agathos* means "good," as in a "morally good" person. That is not the Greek word used here. It is the other word for "good," *kalos* as in "good at" something. Jesus was not just a "good person, he was good at shepherding." In short, he was "good" and "good at it."

It occurred to me that these two Greek words for "good," *agathos* and *kalos* are the two qualities that we all need. No matter what profession we follow or vocation we answer, like the Good Shepherd, we need to be "good" and "good at it," not one or the other, but both together.

We must be *agathos*, good people, authentic human beings aware of who we are, in control of ourselves, aware of our place in the human family and committed to our own spiritual and personal growth. Those of us who follow Christ must hunger and thirst for the holiness of Jesus, himself, not in some obnoxious, pious, religious-fanatic way, but in a whole human person kind of way.

But it is not enough just to be *agathos*, a "good person," we must also be "good at what we do." As a priest I am hopefully committed to being a good person, but I must also commit to developing my skills at preaching, celebrating the sacraments and leading faith communities. Like the Good Shepherd, I cannot not just be personally "good," I must also be "good at shepherding." Those of you who will marry must know that you cannot make a good couple without both partners being individually good people. Even then, you must not just be individually good, you must be good at being a partner and later be good at parenting. If you become teachers or nurses you must be more than "good people," you must be good at teaching and competent at nursing. Whatever your profession or vocation, to be really successful, you must dedicate yourselves to "being good" and "good at what you do."

No matter how professionally competent we are, we must also be good people at the base. No matter how good of a person we are at base, we must be competent at what we do. This is a whole person, a holy person, an integrated, fully-man person, balancing love of God, love of self and love of others. Bellarmine has tried to do that for you, turn you out as good people and competent people, professionally. If I may quote from the mission statement of Bellarmine University, "Bellarmine is a university where talented and diverse persons of all faiths and ages develop the intellectual, moral and professional competencies to lead, to serve, and to make a living and a life worth living." "Making a living and a life worth living" is another way of saying, "now it's time to get out there and be *agathos* and *kalos*."

Choose, But Choose Wisely

May 8, 2004

I have set before you life and death, the blessing and the curse. Choose life, then, that you and your descendants may live, by loving the Lord your God, heeding his voice and holding fast to him.

DEUTERONOMY 30: 19,20

Do you want what's behind door number one, door number two or door number three? Do you want to keep the new kitchen appliances that you have already won or would you like to trade them for what's behind the curtain on stage? Some of you may remember the long-running TV show, "Let's Make a Deal." Contestants in ridiculous costumes were offered choices between "a bird in the hand or two in the bush," between what was certain and what was possible. Sometimes people would trade something like a plastic comb for a choice of doors. Sometimes they would end up with a Hawaiian vacation, a room full of furniture or a booby prize. The biggest winners were confronted with a second, more difficult choice. They were asked whether they wanted to trade their Hawaiian vacation for what was behind a curtain. They could win a shiny new car or they could end up with a live jackass.

The program was popular, I believe, because it was symbolic of the human predicament. We, especially you graduates, are faced with a world of choices and sometimes those choices produce great blessings and sometimes they bring disasters. Sometimes we will be better off because of our good choices and sometimes we will have to live in a hell of regret because of our bad choices, knowing that we brought ruin on ourselves because of those bad choices.

In the first reading chosen for this Mass, the Israelites are about to enter the "promised land" after an arduous trip across the Sinai desert. Before they start their exciting new lives in the land of plenty, Moses lectures them about the necessity of make good choices in a land filled with blessings and curses as well. Their happiness will depend, in a great measure, on how they choose to choose.

In many ways you graduates are entering a "promised land flowing with milk and honey" after having survived the arduous journey of college and you, too, have choices to make. Your choices will affect you for good or for bad. You need to know that your freedom to choose does not guarantee that you will make good choices. Making good choices requires, not just knowledge and freedom, but wisdom. You live in a world of unprecedented knowledge on one hand and unprecedented lack of wisdom on the other. The ability to choose from many choices does not guarantee that you will choose wisely. The world you are entering is full of smart people doing a whole lot of dumb things. You know a lot of facts and you have been pumped full of information, but at the same time you are entering a world knee-deep in the fall-out of people's bad choices. The freedom to choose from a smorgasbord of choices does not guarantee that you will choose wisely.

It is important that you are not just smart, but wise. It is important that you choose wisely because your choices will bring blessing on you and those around you or they can bring ruin on you and the rest of us as well.

This brings me to another point. You were not created nor have you been educated merely for your own good. As Jesus says to his followers in the gospel reading today, "No one lights a lamp and puts it under a bushel basket or under a bed; he puts it on a lampstand so that whoever comes in can see it," and in another place, "You are the salt of the earth and the light of the world. Your light must shine."

I would like to end this short homily by quoting Nelson Mandela, who quoted Marriane Williamson, in his first inaugural speech. I can think of nothing better to leave you with than these challenging words.

> "Our deepest fear is not that we are inadequate. Our deepest fear is that we are powerful beyond measure. It is our light, not our darkness, that most frightens us. There is nothing enlightened about shrinking so that other people won't feel secure around you. You were born to make manifest the glory of God that is within us. It's not just in some of us. It's in everyone. And as we let our own light shine, we unconsciously give others permission to do the same. As we are liberated from our own fear, our presence automatically liberates others."

Graduates, make good choices and let your light shine – for your own good and the good of the world in which you will live, work and raise your children, and, yes, the world the rest of us will be living in as well! We need you to be good and good at what you do. God is there to help you and we are here to support you. Congratulations, good luck and may God be with you!

Be Well Connected

May 14, 2005

*Like a tree planted near running water, whose
leaves never fade. Like a house built on rock, able
to withstand a ragging storm.*
JEREMIAH 11 AND MATTHEW 7

Laptop computers, palm pilots, Blackberries, iPods,
MP3 players, cell phones, digital cameras, DVD players:
these are a few of the many technological gadgets that are
now available for the taking. Personally, I am a bit techno-
logically challenged. I say "a bit" because I *do* have a computer, a cell phone and a digital camera. My latest discovery,
the most useful gadget of all next to my computer, is my
portable Magellan Road Mate Global Positioning System.

Part of my job as the Director of the "Institute for
Priests and Presbyterates" over at Saint Meinrad, is to trav-
el to many of the dioceses served by Saint Meinrad School
of Theology. I fly to some, but I drive to many. One of the
things that worried me when I started this job was driving
around these strange cities, by myself, while trying to read
a map. Thanks to my GPS all I have to do is plug it into my
cigarette lighter, turn it on, wait a minute or two until it
connects to a series of twelve satellites, punch in an address
and it displays the route and verbally directs me right to the
door. Even if I make a wrong turn, it immediately tells me
so and directs me back to where I needed to turn in the
beginning.

It occurred to me the other day that a GPS is amazingly analogous to our lives as a disciples of Jesus. A disciple regularly "logs on" to Jesus through prayer to receive direction and clarity in staying on the right track in living his or her life. As Isaiah, the prophet, put it: "A voice shall sound in your ear, 'This is the way; walk in it,' when you would turn this way or that."

This is my 299th Bellarmine homily. That's a lot of preaching. So far, I have not run out of things to preach about. I know it sounds a bit overly pious, maybe even corny, but I never begin a homily without reminding myself that the God who called me to this task stands by to help me. When I am "connected," so to speak, ideas seem to flow freely, sometimes faster than I can write them down. Preparing to preach is never magic, but I often feel as if I am being helped and guided.

Whenever I get lost and lose my way, like I did two years ago during the worst days of the clergy abuse scandal, I find that I need to put myself in the presence of God so as to get some direction and clarity. At the beginning of 2004 I took some time off and went to a beach house by myself for a whole month to be with God and to get some clarity. It worked. I got my direction. I got my clarity. I got back on my path and went from one of the worst years of priesthood to one of the best.

A Global Positioning System is just a symbolic, if not too simple way to explain our connection to the helping and guiding presence of God in our lives. The ancients had other ways of describing this same helping and guiding presence of God. They compared it to being like a tree planted near running water and a house built on rock. Unlike a tree planted in a desert, a tree planted near running water stays green, no matter how severe the drought, because it is connected by its roots to a constant supply of fresh water. Unlike a house built on sand, a house built on rock never has to worry about storms because it is solidly anchored. These readings contain the truth of this simple message, a message that can be very helpful to those of you graduating today.

Whether you are graduating from the business school, the school of education, the health sciences school or any of the other schools for that matter; whether you are married, become a parent, go for another degree, own your own business or run for office; the best way to live is to build your house on solid rock and plant yourself by running water so that, by having depth, you can survive all of life's storms and droughts – not only survive, but thrive as a healthy, whole human person, created in the image and likeness of God. The glory of God is man or woman fully alive.

At Saint Meinrad we try to form future priests in four areas: human growth, intellectual growth, professional growth and spiritual growth. These four pillars of personal growth are useful for everybody. As graduates, you too are called to honor God by continually growing as a human being, by continuing to use your mind, by becoming more and more competent at what you do and, yes, by tapping into God's strength and being anchored to him.

Organized religion is taking its punches these days, but organized religion is just an earthenware jar that holds a great treasure. Don't be so put off by the earthenware jar that you miss the great treasure that it holds. The institutional church will always be in need of reform, but look beyond its imperfect structure to the community of believers that it holds together. Find a community of faith and stay connected, so that you can feed others and be fed by them. The church is more than just a flawed institution, it is the very Body of Christ acting in our world through us. Come back to it when you lose your way, when you get lost. It's a tough world out there. Be like a tree planted near running water. Be like a house built on rock If you do that you won't have to worry about droughts and storms. You can stand tall even on the worst days!

Be Good Seeds

May 13, 2006

Some seeds were eaten by birds, some withered under the sun, some were choked by weeds, but some grew into a huge harvest.

MARK 4 1-9

One of the things about being a priest of my age is that you are always running into people you have baptized or united in marriage several years back. Often you are amazed at how far they have come. Sometimes, however, you are shocked by how far some beautiful young couples have let themselves go! Sometimes it's all you can do to hold back a gasp. The same can be said about priests. The years have not been kind to them. They are like sprouted seedlings scalded by the sun or growing plants crowded by weeds. They squandered their potential. It hurts too much to watch.

What got them into trouble in the first place, I believe, is their belief that things like graduations, weddings and ordinations mark the end of school, the end of dating and the end of seminary instead of a beginning – a beginning of a lifetime of fighting one's lazy streak and one's temptation to rest on one's laurels.

Today is called "a commencement" for a reason. Rather than being a celebration of the end of your studies, it is a celebration of the beginning of your careers and lives as independent people. What happens after you leave here is more important than what happened while you were here.

23

We are not celebrating a harvest today. We celebrate the fact that the seeds of your future have finally been planted. What happens next is what really matters.

Jesus makes a very important point in today's gospel: planted seeds, no matter how good they are, must be tended: watered, protected, encouraged with fertilizer and sometimes, even pruned. Otherwise, their potential for reaching their goals will be wasted, stunted or overpowered.

Of course, Jesus was originally talking about the reception his teaching was getting. Some, he said, heard what he said, but evil came and grabbed it like hungry birds gobbling up seeds on top of the ground. Some heard what he said and got all excited at first, but they soon fell away because it required too much. Some heard what he said and listened with enthusiasm, but other things grabbled their attention and soon they lost interest. A few heard what he said, took it in and watched it change their lives forever.

These words can also be applied to you. Some of you will take what you were taught, religiously and academically, and it will be wasted like seeds sprinkled on concrete. It will go nowhere. The investment in you will be wasted. Some of you will take what you were taught and leave here all excited about what you can become, but you will give into your lazy side and do nothing with what was invested in you. Some of you will take what you were taught here and make a great start only to get distracted and side-lined, losing sight of your goals until it is too late to get back on track. Some of you will shock and surprise yourselves and others by taking what you were taught here and parlaying it into a future rich in spiritual/personal development and worldly accomplishment.

The "good seeds" of a Bellarmine education have been planted in each of you, but no matter how good these seeds are, much depends on you, the ground that received them. Today's "most likely to succeed" could be the biggest failures in life, while today's "least likely to succeed" could actually be the biggest success. Nothing is guaranteed. A lot depends on your attitude and willingness to water, protect, encourage and prune what has been planted in you.

Anybody can plant a garden, but what happens after you plant it determines whether you will have delicious vegetables to eat in the future. Just so, many manage to graduate from college, but what happens after graduation determines whether you will turn what you have learned into a satisfying life in the years to come.

Many of our heroes have said as much. Jesse Owens said, "We all have dreams, but in order to make dreams into reality, it takes an awful lot of determination, dedication, self-discipline and effort." Johann von Goethe said, "Knowing is not enough; we must apply. Willing is not enough; we must do." Henry Ward Beecher said, "Hold yourself responsible for a higher standard than anybody else expects of you. Never excuse yourself. Never pity yourself. Be a hard master to yourself – and be lenient to everybody else." John Atkinson said, "If you don't run your own life, somebody else will." Orison Swett Marden said, "The greatest thing a man can do in this world is to make the most possible out of the stuff that has been given him. This is success, and there is no other." And my favorite of all are the words of George Bernard Shaw, "People are always blaming their circumstances for what they are. I don't believe in circumstances. The people who get on in this world are the people who get up and look for circumstances they want, and, if they can't find them, make them. ... This is the true joy in life ... the being a force of nature instead of a feverish selfish clod of ailments and grievances complaining that the world will not devote itself to making you happy."

Graduates! God has used many people to plant the seeds of your future in you. These seeds are God's graduation gift to you. They are God's stake in your future. Seeds represent potential, but potential is nothing unless it is developed. "Knowing is not enough, you must apply. Willing is not enough, you must do." Do not let these precious seeds fall on hard ground, thin ground or weedy ground. Give them a rich, loose soil. Give them plenty of sunshine and water. Bring them to harvest so that you too can take your turn in planting good seeds in those who follow you: you children, your spouse, your community, your church and your world. Then, one day, you can stand in front of your Maker and hear this: "Well done, good and faithful servant!"

Create Yourself

May 12, 2007

*Ask and it will be given to you; seek and you will
find; knock and the door will be opened to you.*
MATTHEW 7: 7

The greatest thing that ever happened to me was not
being ordained to priesthood. The greatest thing that ever
happened to me happened on a fire escape when I was a
senior in college. It was so life changing that I often cringe
when I think about how my life might be today if it had not
happened. I have probably told it too many times, but it
seems someone is helped each time I tell it.

At that time I was bashful, backward and scared of life.
I might describe my philosophy of life up to that point as
"life is something that happens *to* you and all you can do is
make the most of it." I felt powerless. I felt like a victim of
circumstances. I was what George Bernard Shaw called "a
feverish selfish little clod of ailments and grievances complaining that the world would not devote itself to making
me happy." I was so scared of life that I spent most of my
energy avoiding new people, new circumstances, new pos-
sibilities and new ideas. I did the minimum. I avoided challenges. I was so bashful that I could not read in front of
people, much less stand up here and talk to a group like
this. I was actually quite creative in my efforts to be sure
that I was never in an uncomfortable situation. I worked
very hard to keep the world at bay. As a result of all these

efforts I finally had to admit that I was miserable, miserable indeed!

Between classes that day, I was standing on a fire escape – the only place we could smoke back then – when all of a sudden I blurted out to my best friend standing there with me, "Pat! I am so damned tired of being bashful, backward and scared of life, I am going to do something about it even if it kills me and I am going to ask God to help me do it!" It was not one of those New Year's resolutions that last a day or two. For the first time in my life, it was not just a wish. It was a decision. I decided to grab life by the horns.

Again, in the words of George Bernard Shaw, I had discovered one of life's greatest principles. "Life isn't about finding yourself. Life is about creating yourself." I decided to stand up to my own cowardice. I decided to be a "force of nature" instead of a "feverish little clod of ailments and grievances." I had an excuse for everything because I believed that I was a victim of circumstances. I was born in a small town. I didn't have any money. I never had anyone to help me … on and on and on! That day I decided to quit blaming circumstances, to quit whining and create my own circumstances. Again it is George Bernard Shaw who described what I decided to do that day on the fire escape. "People are always blaming their circumstances for what they are. I don't believe in circumstances. The people who get on in this world are the people who get up and look for the circumstances they want, and, if they can't find them, make them."

Again, I am reminded of something I saw on TV many years ago. It reminds me of myself and many other people that I have met over the years. I was watching TV one day. There was a handsome young man, about the age of many of you. He was involved in a tragic accident that left him with only one of his legs. He was sitting in a wheel chair complaining about how unfair life had been to him, how he life was over and how nothing good was ever possible for him again. It was depressing so I changed the channel. There on the screen was another handsome young man coming down the mountain on skis, snow flying everywhere as he made his way down the mountain. It wasn't until he got to the bottom of the hill that I realized he was a one-legged skier competing in the Handicapped Olympics. They were both missing a leg, but one young man gave up and the other got up!

The decision I made that day on the fire escape was not magic. Most of my praying up until then was more like wishing things would be different. A wish changes nothing. A decision changes everything. In the words of Jesus in his teaching on prayer, I had to "ask," "seek," and "knock." Those words are action words. Once I got out of the back seat of life and got behind the wheel, my prayers were *indeed* answered. I "received." I "found" and "the door was opened" for me.

That decision was instant, but it took years of facing my fears, one fear at a time, to get where I am today. I am still working my program. I still place myself deliberately in painful situations that offer me a chance to grow into new areas of life. When I start getting comfortable, I do what I call "induce labor." I set out in a new direction and go through the painful process of growth over and over again. I hope to do this until I am dead.

Graduates! Besides working here at Bellarmine on the weekends, I teach another group of 19 young adults at St. Meinrad Seminary – those who are about to be ordained priests from around the United States. My class is about the transition out of seminary and into pastoral ministry. My question to them is this – "now that you will be a priest, what kind of priest do you will to be?" I remind them that ordination is not magic. Using the words of Pope John Paul II, "all formation is ultimately self-formation," I try to teach them that life is about facing down their our own fears and laziness so as to create the kind of priest they need to be.

Graduates! I have preached a lot of baccalaureates, performed a lot of weddings and attended a lot of ordinations in the last thirty-seven years. One of the things all these celebrations have in common is the belief held by many of those going through them – that they have finally finished – finished with classes, finished with dating and finished with seminary. They have, in reality, only just begun. Once graduation is over, you have to go back to school or get to work. Once the wedding is over, you have to get busy building a marriages and managing a family. Once ordination is over, you have to get busy serving the needs of people. All of us have to create the life we want, not just sit back and wait for it to be handed to us or blame circumstances for what we have become.

Yes, God is there to help. As the old adage goes, "When the student is ready, the teacher will appear." Prayer is not about passively wishing and hoping things will be different. Prayer is about "asking, seeking and knocking." "For everyone who asks, receives; and the one who seeks, finds; and for the one who knocks, the door will be opened."

Graduates! The words of Saint Paul to his young partner in ministry, Timothy, can also be applied to you. "Do not neglect the gift you have. Attend to yourself and the work given to you. Be diligent in these matters, be absorbed in them, so that your progress may be evident to everyone."

Life, then, is not about "finding yourself." With God's help, life is about "creating yourself," whether you are a graduating senior, a tenured faculty member or an old priest!

Be a Person of Integrity!

May 10, 2008

The person who is trustworthy in very small matters is also trustworthy in great ones; and the person who is dishonest in very small matters is also dishonest in great ones.

LUKE 16:1-10

Trash TV is forever giving some of the weakest people in our culture a spotlight for showing off their crudeness, addictions and ignorance. I must confess that I get sucked into watching it sometimes – usually with a jaw dropped in amazement. Just when you think you've heard and seen it all, the ante is "upped" in one form or another. "Tom, Dick, Harry, John, Kevin, Bob, George, Devin! All eight of you are *not* the father!" "I am here today to tell my teenaged daughter that I have been secretly having a relationship with her boy friend for the last three years!" "I want to come clean today with my girl friend and tell her today that I am the one who has been secretly cashing her grandparents social security checks for the last three years in order to cover my gambling debts."

One of the themes that gets regular coverage is the inability to say "no." Pathetic examples of humanity tell the audience in a million different ways that if the temptation is there, one is forced to give into it because one is surely powerless to do otherwise. Likewise, if the opportunity arises to commit adultery, defraud the government or take something from work, we are told that a person would be foolish to pass it up.

Today's gospel calls us to be people of integrity, no matter what call we have answered. A person of integrity knows right from wrong and has the strength of character to choose what is right, even when no one is looking, even when it is possible to choose wrong and get away with it. The opposite of a person with integrity is a small self-centered person, always "on the make," no matter how devastating the effect is on himself or others.

The ability to say "no" to opportunistic situations is one of the most basic abilities of a person of integrity. A person of integrity declares his independence from the terminal egoism of popular culture. A person of integrity responds to life from well-defined principles, not from his or her basest addictions.

A person of integrity says "no" to the assumption that says "the end justifies the means." When we buy into this perspective, we are willing to use deception, manipulation and even death to accomplish our "good" goals.

A person of integrity says "no" to radical materialism – that driving passion to "own," "possess" and "have" at all cost, even at the expense of individuals and the community as a whole.

A person of integrity says "no" to radical individualism. Radical individualists promote themselves only, always taking and never giving back. We are social beings by nature. We live in communities and are therefore never free to do whatever we wish in an absolute sense.

A person of integrity says "no" to the "group-think," the "herd mentality," "what everybody else is doing." Unable to love themselves, people without integrity are unable to love others. Addicts to the "latest best offer," their marriages often end in tragedy. Refusing to grow up, they do not have what it takes to sustain family life and leave children without the parenting that is rightfully theirs!

Students! If all this sounds terribly counter-cultural, it is! One of the marks of mature adulthood is the ability to do hard things for one's own good, to stand up to the coward in oneself and to say "no" to lazy, destructive choices. Build your life on solid principles, no matter how few follow you.

I teach a class every spring semester to the guys who will be ordained to the priesthood this spring. In fact, they are also going through their own graduations at Saint Meinrad today. They have been though four, six or more years of supervision and evaluations to make sure they are doing what they should be doing. I spend a lot of time preparing them to be their own spiritual directors and life coaches, if need be, because their success, like yours, will depend a great deal on their ability to say "no" to lazy, destructive choices that may *feel good* to them in the short run and say "yes" to the hard choices that are *really good* for them in the long run.

Graduates, the sign that you have really reached adulthood will be your ability to manage your own appetites, your ability to do hard things for your own good, your ability to stand up to that perpetual adolescence that is so popular and embarrassing in so many middle-aged men and women today. Choose the things that will give you life. Reject the things that will bring death into your life. Choose to be directed by solid spiritual principles, rather than always going with the latest best offer, always taking the road most traveled, always choosing the easy way. Be a man or woman of integrity instead of a slave to your own cowardice and addictions. A man or woman of integrity, with a good education, has the ability to be a successful professional, a successful marriage partner, a successful parent, indeed whatever God calls him or her to be.

Let me end this homily with a quote from one of my heroes, Victor Frankl, a prisoner in a Nazi concentration camp.

> "Everything can be taken from a man but one thing, the last of human freedoms, the ability to choose one's attitude in any given set of circumstances, the ability to choose one's own way."

Graduates. Reject "group think." Choose to be directed by spiritual solid principles. Choose to be men and women of integrity.

Attend to Yourself

May 9, 2009

Do not neglect the gift you have. Attend to your-self and to your teaching. Persevere in both tasks.
I TIMOTHY: 4:14-16

I have a small paper copy of a famous "NO WHINING" button taped to my bathroom mirror. It has the word WHINING in a circle with a left to right, line slashing through it.

People who whine, myself or others, whine not only when we are unhappy, but even more so when we expect to be rescued from our unhappiness by others. Whiners feel powerless and believe that if *someone else* would only do this or that, or quit doing this or that, *they themselves* would be happier and more successful.

I keep that sign on my bathroom mirror to remind me each day to take responsibility for my *own* happiness - a decision that I actually made *consciously* for the first time, one spring day very much like this one, back in 1965.

Starting with small baby-steps, I marched out that day to meet life head-on with my mind made up to quit my whin-ing, to start making myself happy and to quit blaming other people and the circumstances of my life for my unhappi-ness. I have made tremendous progress in the last 44 years, but there are still a few cancerous "whining cells" in my bloodstream that manifest themselves every now and then. I keep that "no whining" sign on my bathroom mirror so every morning I am reminded to keep working my program.

Graduates! Imagine, for a moment, what *you* will be like in 2034 – at your 25th class reunion! Will it be a matter of luck or intention? Some of you who struggled through college will be successful beyond your wildest imaginations! Some of you who graduate with honors today will allow that advantage to slip away from you. For most of you, what happens to you between now and then will be of your own making, either by design or neglect. Whether you succeed or fail will depend a lot on *you* – on whether you accept or abdicate responsibility for your own life, instead of blaming other people and circumstances for where you have ended up. Sure, there are *some* circumstances beyond our control, a few tragedies over which we have no power, but I have tried to follow these words of George Bernard Shaw, "People are always blaming their circumstances for what they are. I don't believe in circumstances. The people who get on in this world are the people who get up and look for the circumstances they want, and of they can't find them, make them."

In our first reading today, the young missionary, Timothy, was discouraged by his circumstances, wanted to quit and come home, whining that nobody would listen to him. Timothy must have been a real whiner because Paul has to write to him at least twice. In his first letter he writes this to Timothy. "Let no one have contempt for you because of your youth, but set an example for those who believe. Watch over yourself and over your teaching; persevere in both tasks, for by doing so, you will save both yourself and those who listen to you." (4:12-16) In other words, "Quit whining! You've got important work to do! You're talented. Now go do it. Do what? Take care of yourself and take care of the people entrusted to your care."

In his second letter to the young Timothy, the problem seems to persist because Paul says this to him: "Fan into flame the gift that God gave you at your ordination. God did not give you a spirit of cowardice, but rather of strength, practical helpfulness and courage in the face of tragedy." (1:6-7)

"Timothy! Get a grip! Quit using your youth as an excuse! Attend to yourself and to the people God has entrusted to your care." This advice from Saint Paul is extremely appropriate even today. The one thing that all successful leaders, parents, spouses, professionals and teachers have in common is their passionate drive for improvement – both in who they are and in what they do – a fierce commitment to their own lifelong formation and an unflinching quest for personal excellence. In other words, all successful leaders, parents, priests, nursing professionals, spouses, and teachers are committed to "attending to themselves and attending to those entrusted to their care."

Excellence in pastoral ministry, parenting, marriage, business, health care or teaching is never about watching over either oneself *or* others, but watching over both. A priest who only takes care of himself and neglects his people is a disgrace as a priest, but so is the hard-working priest who never takes care of himself. A spouse who only takes care of himself or herself and neglects his or her spouse and children is a disgrace to marriage, but so also is the marriage partner or parent who is always taking care of others while neglecting him or herself. We must attend to ourselves and those entrusted to us by God and keep them in balance.

In this discipline of watching over oneself and over what one is called to do, I would like to refer to what we call in seminary training, "the four pillars:" human formation, spiritual formation, intellectual formation and professional formation. These "four pillars" are used in our programs for the ongoing formation of priests after seminary as well. Even though they were developed for seminarians and priests, they apply to leaders, professionals, parents, spouses and teachers as well.

To attend to oneself and to one's call, to be good and good at what one does, one must pay attention to one's *human* formation. This means striving to become the best person we can be, as well as increasing one's capacity to relate to others. As Jesus put it, "A bad tree cannot bear good fruit nor can a good tree bear bad fruit." A mess of a human being can never be a good marriage partner, parent, priest, business professional, pastoral worker or teacher. Becoming a good "anything," begins with a whole, healthy human person.

To watch over oneself and over what one is called to do, one must pay attention to one's *spiritual* formation. A good priest must have a vigorous personal spiritual life if he is to be a successful spiritual leader, and a vigorous spiritual life is impossible without regular tending. It has been proven, over and over again in study after study, that marriages that have God in them last longer and are happier than those without God in them. In the Sacraments of Marriage and Baptism, parents are asked if they are willing to accept the responsibility of bringing their children up in the practice of the faith. Parents who are not working on their own spiritual formation will not be able to meet their responsibility as primary teachers of the faith to their children.

To watch over oneself and over what one is called to do, one must pay attention to one's *intellectual* formation. Any good priest, parent, professional, or marriage partner, must be open to growing in wisdom and knowledge in an ever more complex world with its ever evolving scientific and technological discoveries. We need to know what is going on in the world, if we are to engage the world and keep up with it. We must commit to being life-long learners or the world will simply leave us behind.

To watch over oneself and over what one is called to do, one must pay attention to one's *professional* formation. Even though each of us receives a different call in life, none of us is born a good parent, priest, pastoral worker, business or health professional, teacher or spouse. We must constantly sharpen our abilities and develop our skills. As Jesus told us in the parable of the talents, we might each be given different talents, but every one of us is called to *invest* those talents and help them grow. Saint Paul tell Timothy, "not to neglect the gift he has been given, ... but to be diligent in these matters, even absorbed in them ... so that your progress will be evident." "By doing so," he says, "you will save both yourself and those who listen to you."

Students! All of you have been blessed. The challenge ahead of you is to now do something with those blessings. In preparation for your 25th Bellarmine Reunion in 2034, grab the bull by the horns starting today! Accept personal responsibility for yourself. No whining! Cultivate your own drive for improvement – both in who you are *and* in what you do. In the end, life is not about *finding* yourself, but about working with God to *create* yourself.

Be a Good Tree That Bears Good Fruit

May 8, 2010

A good tree bears good fruit and a rotten tree bears bad fruit .

MATTHEW 7:17

Let me join the chorus of people - administration, faculty, family and friends – who congratulate you today on your graduation from Bellarmine University. Indeed, it takes a village to produce a graduate! To celebrate this accomplishment, it is fitting that we gather today to give God thanks for his past support and to ask God for his continued blessings on wherever you go and whatever you do.

This afternoon, as each dean presents your name to the president, he or she will list the skills and competencies that go into earning your particular degree. Many of you will graduate "with honors" because you have displayed incredible skills and competencies.

What I would like to do this morning is to say a few words about the moral and ethical strength you will need to go with those skills and competencies to be truly successful. Surely, we all know from watching the evening news that many people with incredible skills and competencies have crashed and burned because they lack character – they lack moral and ethical strength. Character defects have brought down countless presidents, doctors, lawyers, priests, business men and women, and teachers. Jesus has warned us that no matter how beautiful the house we build may be, if it is built on sand, it is liable to collapse and ruin. He puts it another way in today's gospel, "A rotten tree cannot bear good fruit!"

Graduates, if you want to be truly successful, you will not only need skills and competencies, but also strength of character. To develop our character we have to practice virtue. You might have a degree in psychology and land a job as a counselor, but if you lack prudence, you will have a hard time giving clients sound advice. You might have an MBA and get a job in a major corporation, but if you lack courage, your ability to lead in face of opposition and hard times will be compromised. You might have a degree in theology and snag a job as a director of religious education in one of our parishes, but if you lack self-control you will surely be a menace to yourself and to others and fail miserably. You may find the most perfect marriage partner in the world, but if you lack self-discipline, there is no way you can hope to maintain a happy marriage. "A bad tree simply cannot bear good fruit."

To go with the skills and competencies we acquire, we need to practice those sound moral habits that we call "virtues." Virtues are qualities of the mind, the will and the heart that instill strength of character and stability of personality. They are acquired through constant and deliberate repetition.

The great philosopher, Plato, identified four main human virtues: prudence, justice, courage and self-control. Because the same four are listed in our first reading today, the Book of Wisdom, we can conclude that ancient Jews valued this wisdom from the ancient Greeks. Our first reading puts it this way: "Nothing in life is more useful for mortals than these: moderation, prudence, justice and courage."

Prudence has to do with the ability to make good, sound decisions. We live in a culture where decisions are often made quickly, without solid information and without serious reflection on their consequences. Having good intentions and meaning well, confusing fact and fiction and operating out of our addictions, are not good enough. Prudence requires that we possess the ability to see reality as it is and make sound decisions based on that reality. Running up huge credit card debts through impulse buying and rushing into a marriage without really knowing ourselves or the person we are marrying are indications that we lack prudence and this lack will no doubt create personal misery for us, and those around us, for years to come.

Justice has to do with the ability to give every person his due. No one is an island. We are part of the main. Human beings have social responsibilities – as citizens, as family members and as neighbors. The practice of the virtue of justice allows us to live ordered and predictable lives where we can expect our rights and the rights of those around us, to be respected. Without justice, it's every dog for himself, and in that kind of world we will all descend into a hellish existence in short order.

Courage or *fortitude* has to do with the ability to stay on course no matter what. Courage enables us to endure the hardships of life, strengthens our resolve to resist the temptations to give up or give in and helps us keep our eyes fixed on what is truly important. Courage does not make us immune from fear, but gives us the ability to overcome it for a higher purpose.

Self-control or *temperance* has to do with the ability to subordinate our passions for the sake of a higher purpose.

Self-control enables us to moderate our attraction to pleasure and provides balance in the use of the world's goods. Food is good, but to eat everything and anything in sight is a perfect way to ruin one's health and to limit one's options in other areas. Sex is good, but to have sex with anyone at anytime is a perfect way to ruin a great relationship, a solid marriage, a good family and even our health. Money is good, but to be fixated on it and to acquire it through any means or methods is a perfect way to end up in poverty, shame and loneliness.

Graduates, your graduation could take you places where your character cannot sustain you. To go with the tremendous skills and competencies you have learned here at Bellarmine, continue to develop your character through the consistent practice of these virtues. Just as a "bad tree cannot bear good fruit," it's just as true that a "good tree cannot bear bad fruit." Build your house, not on the sands of whims, self-indulgence, spiritual indifference, compulsions and addictions which will lead to personal ruin, but build it on the solid rock of a disciplined and virtuous life that will enable you to translate your dreams into reality. Good luck and may God continue to bless you!

Discern! Discern! Discern!

May 14, 2011

My prayer is that you may be able to discern what is of value.

PHILIPPIANS 1

One of my hobbies is writing, but when I decided to major in English in college, I was not moving toward something, but away from something. We were required to have enough credits for a major in Philosophy and Classical Languages. I, however, was not about to go through life with that on my record! I took extra credits in English so that I could at least have a degree that I might find useful somewhere. I had no idea at the time that I would end up writing so much, much less have anything published!

One of the things I have developed over forty years of writing is a respect for the power of the *right* word, the *precise* word, the *exact* word. As I reflected on the three words that are being thrown around this weekend – graduation, commencement and baccalaureate – I tried to discern which of them is the *right* word, the *precise* word, the *exact* word to fit this event. The word *baccalaureate* places the emphasis too much on the past, on an ending. The word *commencement* places the emphasis too much on the future, on a new beginning. The word *graduation* places an equal emphasis on the past and the future.

I believe, then, the *right* word, the *precise* word, the *exact* word for your experience this weekend is graduation, with its emphasis on *moving to a new level*, with its emphasis, not on a break, but a continuous *building upon* what has happened during your time at Bellarmine. Pope John Paul II may have captured best what you are called to today when he said, "Remember the past with gratitude, live in the present with enthusiasm and look forward to the future with confidence."

In my other job, I teach young men who are about to be ordained to the priesthood. They, too, are graduating this morning over in Indiana. Over the last semester we have discussed many issues involved in making the transition from seminary into ministry. We have talked about the need to express gratitude to all those who have helped them, the need to forgive those who have disappointed them, how to manage their personal finances, how to manage their time, maintain appropriate personal boundaries, develop healthy life-giving relationships, how to engage in life-long self-formation in their area of expertise and how to enter their first ministry situation with respect and reverence.

In our final class, I left them with a challenge and a prayer. I would like to leave you with the same challenge and prayer. Your transition is not as different from theirs as you might imagine.

My challenge is for you to grab the bull by the horns and take responsibility for yourself and your future. To do that you must be able to stand up to whatever part of a lazy coward that might be within you and discipline yourself to do hard things for your own good. This challenge can best be summed up in four of my favorite quotes. The first two are from George Bernard Shaw. I use them all the time. The reason I like them is they challenge a common belief that was popular when I was growing up and a belief that I see lived out around me each and every day. That belief is that "life is something that happens to you and all you can do is make the most of it." This belief creates "victims" who are always blaming others for their condition.

Shaw challenges that belief, first of all, when he said, "This is the true joy in life, the being used for a purpose recognized by yourself as a mighty one; the being thoroughly worn out before you are thrown on the scrap heap; the being a force of nature instead of a feverish, selfish little clod of ailments and grievances complaining that the world will not devote itself to making you happy." In another place, Shaw said it more succinctly. "Life," he said, "is not about finding yourself. Life is about creating yourself."

Pope John Paul II agreed when he said, "All formation is ultimately self-formation." Bob Dylan had his own way of saying it when he sang, "If you are not busy being born, you are busy dying."

Graduates, again my challenge to you is to grab the bull by the horns and take responsibility for yourself and the life you want. Don't go through life complaining from the back seat. Get behind the wheel!

My prayer for my seminarian class and for you is found in our first reading today – in Saint Paul's Letter to the Christian community of Philippi. "May you be able to discern what is of value." Like the citizens of Philippi, a great commercial center, a crossroads, where every imaginable idea, custom and habit competed for acceptance, you too live in world where every imaginable idea, custom and habit competes for your acceptance. Some are good, some bad and some are downright deadly.

One of the benefits of being a young adult is finally being able to enjoy the freedom to choose. One of the upsides of the freedom to choose is the possibility of building one's life the way one wants through a series of well-thought out personal choices. One of the downsides of the freedom to choose is the possibility of ruining one's life through a series of poorly thought out choices. Some graduates will be able to handle their freedom. They are able to discern what is of value, choose it and parlay it into an incredible life. Others will sadly not be able to handle their freedom. Unable to discern what is of value, they will choose only what feels good in the moment, ending up being forced to live in a self-created hell of regret.

Graduates, today is *your* day. "Carpe diem" – Seize the day! "Be a force of nature not a complaining little clod of grievances and ailments." "Discern what is of value" and develop the self-discipline to grab onto what is of value. Do not be like the maiden and the judge, living in regret, in Whittier's poem, Maude Miller, of whom it was said: "For of all sad words of tongue or pen, the saddest of these: It might have been!" Know that freedom and responsibility go together. Choose freedom and the responsibility that goes with it. By doing that, you will be able to "discern what is of value" and create the life you want to live rather than one you are forced to live!

Plant Yourself Carefully

May 12, 2012

One who puts his trust in God is like a tree planted by the waterside that thrusts its roots to the stream: when heat come it feels no alarm, its foliage stays green; it has no worries in a year of drought and never ceases to bear fruit.

JEREMIAH 17:8

I have two jobs. At Saint Meinrad Seminary and School of Theology I am a pastoral theology teacher and the director of its Continuing Education department. Here, at Bellarmine University, I am director of Catholic Worship within the Campus Ministry department under Melanie Prejean Sullivan. Both Melanie and I are graduates of Saint Meinrad. Both institutions are having their graduations today. I dumped them for you!

You might think that these two institutions have nothing in common – a seminary like that and a university like this – but in reality they have a lot in common.

The word "seminary" comes from the Latin word for "seed." A seminary is a place where seeds are germinated and plants are propagated for transplantation – a greenhouse, if you will. By their very natures, a university and a seminary are, in their own way, temporary, protected, controlled and intensely monitored environments where budding plants are nurtured until they are mature enough to survive transplantation and thrive in normal growing environments.

In the horticultural world, the transition from a protected environment to a normal growing environment requires careful attention. If plants are immature or the environment is harsh, this transition can cause the plants to go into shock. When in shock, plants often quit growing and become susceptible to disease. All plants experience some degree of shock when they undergo transplantation, but when the shock is too much, plants often die. Like so, not all graduates from the seminary are successful in ministry nor do all graduates from universities become successful in their fields after graduation. Much depends on a successful transition from protected, controlled and intensely monitored environments to the normal growing environment of the real world.

The day that marks this transplanting is called a "commencement!" Rather than the emphasis being on the end of your preparation, the emphasis is more accurately on the *beginning* of your careers and lives as independent people. You have accomplished much getting to this point, but even more is riding on where you choose to plant yourself, and care for yourself, after you leave here.

The readings have so much to teach you about this "handing off," "this transition," this "transplantation." They speak of the importance of wisely choosing the environment where you wish to plant yourself and the importance of building your future on a solid foundation.

Our first reading, from the Prophet Jeremiah, compares two possible choices of places to be transplanted. You can transplant yourself into a "lava waste," "a salty, empty patch of earth" and end up a "barren bush that enjoys no change of season" or you can transplant yourself "beside running water" so that your roots can stretch underground into its life giving waters. Planted in a barren lava waste your life will no doubt be harsh and unproductive, but planted near running water with a strong root system, you will not suffer distress even in times of drought; your leaves will always stay green and you will produce fruit. Where and how you choose to "put down roots" makes a difference – a big difference!

In our gospel reading, Jesus uses another image to say pretty much the same thing. Instead of an image from the horticultural world he uses one from the world of architecture. Instead of comparing an undesirable and desirable spot to be transplanted, he talks about an undesirable and desirable spot to build a house. "A fool," he says, "builds his house on sand. When the rains fall, the floods come and the wind blows, a house built on such a shaky foundation will collapse and be totally ruined." "A wise builder," he says, "builds her house on rock." "When the rains fall, the floods come and the winds blow, a house built on such a solid foundation will stand strong and survive storms." Whatever you choose as a foundation for building your lives makes a difference – a big difference!

Graduates! With the support of your family and friends, the faculty and staff of this University and many generous donors, you have been nurtured in this temporary, protected, controlled and intensely monitored environment. Now you are now ready to be transplanted into the real world to grow and become all that you can be. Choose wisely where you choose to plant yourself. You have been given the skills and the materials to build a life of your own design. Choose wisely the foundation on which you choose to build!

Graduates! We live in a society and a time in history when personal choice is seen as a "right." Just as "freedom" must be paired with "responsibility," "good sense" must be paired with "choice." "Stupidity" paired with "choice" spells disaster and it is a sure path to the loss of your ability to choose. In other words, we have the freedom to choose, but we also have the responsibility to choose wisely.

One of the choices you have to make is whether to maintain or abandon the faith of your upbringing. Plant yourself next to God and let your roots grow underground toward his life-giving waters. Planted there, you will be able to stay green and bear fruit, no matter the weather around you. Rooted in Him, you will be able to survive the droughts that will inevitably come your way. Build your lives on the solid foundation of a life of faith. Those of you with a strong faith can weather even the most severe of storms that will inevitably come your way.

Celebrating the Eucharist on your graduation day, like we are doing here this morning, makes great sense to me. "Eucharist" is a Greek word meaning "to give thanks." Another word for the bread that we will break and share is "Viaticum." "Viaticum" comes from Latin words for the bread that you "take with you" to nourish you on your trip. You have a lot to be thankful for today and you will need God's strength in the months and years ahead.

God bless you! Good luck! In the words of Saint Paul, "Test everything! Retain what is good. Discard everything that is evil."

Be Careful How You Build

May 11, 2013

Each one must be careful how he builds.
I CORINTHIANS 3:10-17

Aware that I am bombarded every day with messages about how I ought to live, what I need to choose and what I need to do, I deliberately collect insightful quotations, wise sayings and other tidbits of wisdom and paste them everywhere to remind myself that I am in charge of my own thinking, and not the victim of what "everybody else" is doing or thinking.

On one wall, where I can see it often is this George Bernard Shaw quote. "Life isn't about finding yourself. Life is about creating yourself." This might not mean much to some of you, but for me it symbolizes the greatest break-through in thinking that I have made in my life. Until I was a junior in college, I used to believe that "life was something that happens to you and all you can do is make the most of it." I was what the same George Bernard Shaw called, "a selfish, feverish little clod of grievances and ailment complaining that the world would not get together to make me happy." One day, in a flash of grace, I made the firm decision to quit whining from the back seat of my own life and to get behind the wheel! I know I have told my story hundreds of times, but I also know that every time I tell it, it always inspires someone to make a similar shift in thinking. I am hoping that it will help someone here today who needs to make a shift in his or her thinking away from victimhood toward self-empowerment.

Graduates! The readings today are about the importance of building on a solid foundation, but before you even consider foundations, you must understand and accept the fact that you are the builder of your own life. If you build your life on the rock-solid foundation of sound thinking that leads to good choices, if you "get it" that life is about creating yourself, you will most probably thrive. If, however, you build your life on the sand of weak thinking and lazy choices, you will surely doom yourself to live in a swamps of regrets and "might have beens." St. Paul was right on target when he said, "Each one must be careful how he builds." Jesus was right on target when he said, "If you build your house on rock, it will stand – come hell or high water, but if you build your house on sand, it will collapse when floods roll over it and high winds pound against it."

Most of you are familiar with the monk, Thomas Merton. We have his library here at Bellarmine University. People come from far and wide to use it and absorb his wisdom. Many of you may not be as familiar with the founder of his religious community, the Cistercians, a man named Bernard of Clairvaux. St. Bernard was a great reformer in the Church of the 12th century. He might have died 860 years ago, but his wisdom lives on and it is valuable even today – even for you. He offers you four foundation pillars on which to build a good life. He says you must (a) consider yourself (b) consider those below you (c) consider those around you and (d) consider Him who is above you.

(1) In considering yourself, St Bernard said, "Behold what you are! It is a monstrous thing to see such

dignity trivialized and squandered!" The first foundation stone on which to build a successful life is a passionate commitment to personal excellence – becoming the best version of yourself that you can create with God's help. I learned a little maxim in Latin many years ago which I have found to be so true. *Nemo dat quad non habet* – one cannot give what one does not have. Jesus said, "A bad tree cannot bear good fruit." St. Francis de Sales said, "Be who you are and be that well." In practical terms, if you are going to marry, be good at it, be a fabulous partner or don't get married. If you are going to have kids, be good at it, be a tremendous parent or don't have them. If you are going to go into public service, be good at it, be transparent, honest and self-giving or don't get into it at all. If you are going to a priest, get serious about it or don't get ordained. Be who you say you are. Be a person of integrity. Do the right thing even when no one is looking.

(2) In considering those below you, you must never forget that the gifts you have been given have been given to you, not just for your own good and personal benefit, but for the good of the community. The second foundation stone on which to build a successful life is a passionate commitment to vocational excellence, to be the very best you can be at what you do. This means a lifelong commitment to honing your skills, deepening your respect and reverence for those under your charge and trying always to lift the vision of others to higher sights, their performance to a higher standard and their personalities beyond their normal limitations.

(3) In considering those around you, take stock of those with whom you surround yourself. The third foundation stone on which to build a successful life is to choose your friends and associates wisely. Many people do not realize the impact the type of people with which they surround themselves has on their well-being. These people will either lift you up or bring you down, support you or criticize you, motivate you or drain you. By developing relationships with those committed to constant improvement and the pursuit of the best that life has to offer, you will have plenty of company on your path to the top of whatever mountain you seek to climb. Remember, people who tell you what you want to hear are not necessarily your friends, just as those who tell you what you don't want to hear are not necessarily your enemies. Surround yourself with people of integrity and quality. Do not hang out with lazy thinkers and undisciplined people. Instead of building you up they will bring you down.

(4) Last of all, in considering Him who is above you, never forget where you came from and where you are going. You have not always been here and you will not always be here. In the whole scheme of things, your life span is relatively short. The fourth and final foundation stone on which to build a successful life, therefore, is to develop an interior spiritual life to match your external material life, so that you can walk on two legs, not one. Statistically, marriages with God in them last longer and are happier. The same can probably be said of other vocations and professions. Awareness of God reminds us every day that we are part of something bigger than

ourselves, that an amazing amount of invisible support is just a prayer away and that our lives have a point and a purpose beyond financial success. Don't let religion's many failures cause you to miss out on religion's many contributions.

Students! These four foundation stones, if built upon with care, focus and determination, make up the cornerstones of a good life, in whatever direction you go. Bellarmine has given you an excellent foundation on which to build. Now heed the words of Saint Paul, "Each one of you must be careful how he builds." Remember the words of George Bernard Shaw, "Life is about creating yourself." You have the freedom and tools to make something of yourself. Rise to the challenge. What you do with the freedom and tools given you is up to you. I pray that each of you will develop a passionate commitment both to "who you are" and "what you do." I pray that you will seek to be good and good at it. If you commit to doing these things, you should do well, whatever mountain you choose to climb. Last of all, when you are successful, remember Bellarmine and help those behind you, just as those in front of you have helped you. Good luck and God bless you!

Make Your Bucket List Now

May 8, 2015

Hold to deliberation and planning. They will be life to your soul. Then you may go your way securely and your foot will never stumble.

PROVERBS 3

Over the Christmas holidays last year I watched the 2007 movie, "The Bucket List," starring Morgan Freeman and Jack Nicholson. It's about two terminally ill old men on a road trip with a list of things to do before they "kick the bucket."

In one of my very favorite scenes, they are both sitting on one of the pyramids in Egypt. Morgan Freeman's character says to Jack Nicholson's character, "You know the ancient Egyptians had a beautiful belief about death. When their souls got to the entrance to heaven … the gods asked them two questions. Their answer determined whether they were admitted or not. 'Have you found joy in your life? Has your life brought joy to others?'"

Today, I want to talk to you about making your bucket list now, not waiting until you are at the end of your life. If you are going to answer the two questions from the movie, in any degree of enthusiasm and reality, you must develop a plan and work that plan till you die – even if you have to make revisions along the way. To paraphrase an exchange between Alice and the Cheshire Cat in Lewis Carroll's *Alice in Wonderland*, "If you don't know where you're going any road will take you there."

I believe in this practice so much that I actually wrote a book on it for the young guys I teach at the seminary over in Indiana. It is called *Personal Growth Plan: A Handbook for Priests*. I challenge them to proceed into priesthood with the end in mind. I ask them where they would like to end up, spiritually, financially and psychologically. I remind them that if they want to end up there they need to start planning now. As part of the financial section of the personal growth plan, I give them each $100 to open individual retirement accounts and tell them not to trust the Church or anyone else to take care of them when they are old – even if they are "supposed to." To show them how right I am, I refer to a February survey of diocesan priests' retirement plans that reveals that a majority of US diocesan priests' retirement plans are underfunded. They could be left stranded after a lifetime of ministry unless they act now!

It has been said that most people who reach 65 or beyond, look back on their lives with regret. They wish they had set their priorities differently. Choices made, whether bad or good, follow us forever and affect everyone in our paths, one way or another. As far as that goes, not to choose *is* a choice. Not to choose is a choice! If we want a new tomorrow, then we have to make new choices today. Not every fairy tale story that begins with "Once upon a time," has a "happily ever after" ending. J. K Rowling said, "There is an expiration date on blaming your parents for steering you in the wrong direction; the moment you are old enough to take the wheel, responsibility lies with you." There is nothing better in life than commitment to personal development and lifelong learning. Our lives are the sum result of all the choices we make, both consciously and unconsciously. If we can control the process of choosing, we can take more control of more aspects of our lives.

There is a certain freedom that comes from being in charge of ourselves.

"Have you found joy in your life?" "Has your life brought joy to others?" If you are going to be able to answer those questions with conviction – fifty, sixty or seventy years in the future – now is the time to start. Our first reading, from the Book of Proverbs, tells us to "hold to deliberation and planning, they will be life to your soul, ... you may go your way securely, your foot will never stumble, ... when you lie down, you will not be afraid and when you rest your sleep will be sweet."

In speaking about discipleship, the passage from the gospel that we read tells us that if we set out to build a tower, we need to first sit down and calculate the cost to see if we have what it takes to finish it. Otherwise, after laying the foundation, we might wake up and realize that we do not have the needed resources to finish. Success is more than a good idea or a sincere wish. What is it about certain people that makes them successful in achieving what they set out to do and reach their greatest potential? Is it luck? Do they have better connections with people of power and influence? Does God have favorites? I don't think so. I believe they have two things: singleness of purpose in where they want to go and the disciplined personal habits that will take them there. Success requires that we have perfect clarity about what we want, constant vigilance to stay on task, regular reevaluation along the way and personal discipline to bring it to completion. "Translating a dream into reality takes great courage. Doubt is a constant enemy. When doubt reigns, there is a strong temptation to let go of part of the dream as a way of resolving inevitable tensions. Success depends on the ability to remain enthusiastic, focused and purposeful to the end."

"Have you found joy in your life?" "Has your life brought joy to others?" The first reading teaches us to be mindful of God and not to think that we are wise enough to do without him. We must love ourselves enough to accept his help because it is he who will "keep our paths straight." Let me be clear here. The self-love I am talking about here is not the same as being selfish. Self-love, more often than not, is about us doing hard things for our own good rather than simply indulging our appetites and addictions. Self-care is not a selfish act – it is simply good stewardship of the only gift we have, the gift of ourselves that we were put on this earth to offer others. Without true love for oneself, without finding joy in our own lives, we will most certainly have nothing of quality to give others – we will not be able to bring joy into their lives either.

Selfishness, on the other hand, is about seeking or con-centrating on one's own advantage, pleasure or well-being without regard for others. Self-absorption in all its forms kills empathy, let alone compassion. When we focus on ourselves, our world contracts as our problems and preoc-cupations loom large. But when we focus on others, our world expands. Our own problems drift to the periphery of the mind and so seem smaller, and we increase our capacity for connection or compassionate action. One Native American Elder made this wise observation. "Inside of me there are two dogs. One of the dogs is mean and evil. The other dog is good. The mean dog fights the good dog all the time." When asked which dog wins, he reflected for a moment and replied, "The one I feed the most."

Graduates! The truth of the matter is this – we were cre-ated in the image and likeness of God. We are temples of the Holy Spirit. We are light and salt to enlighten and give flavor to the world. We are set on a hill to be seen. We have been given talents to invest. We are called to love ourselves and love those around us. We are called to find joy in our lives and bring joy into the lives of others. Nothing else is as important as that. Nothing! If we get that wrong, we have indeed failed at life.

If you want to ruin the great gift of life that has been entrusted to you, if you want to end up in a joyless life and a life that does not contribute joy to anyone around you, just marry the first person you get the "hots" for, just go ahead and try heroin, just post some idiotic self-defeating information on Facebook, just decide not to accept that scholarship for a master or a doctorate because you're tired of school, just go ahead and abuse your credit card until your credit score is zero, just eat as much junk food as you can stuff in your mouth, just have irresponsible sex until someone gets pregnant or contracts some incurable disease, just don't listen to anybody or take anyone's advice –just do whatever feels good, just don't bother to have a plan and go with the flow. We must all suffer one of two things: the pain of discipline or the pain of regret.

If you forgo deliberation and planning and if you fail to develop the personal discipline to go with it, you could find yourself at the end being one of those million "could have beens, might have beens and should have beens." The real losers will be those bitter people who get to the end, still blaming their parents, the times they lived in, the system that was so unfair to them or whatever excuses they can come up with. The truth of the matter is, we have a choice, we can affect the outcome of our lives by creating our bucket list now and practicing the discipline it takes to work through it, without lame excuses, without whining blame and without lazy shortcuts. God is here to help. We can accept it or reject it. You have been given a good education. You can use it or squander it. Ultimately, your choice comes down to this: you can "run with the big dogs or you can just sit on the porch and bark!"